COMPILED BY

GLOUCESTERSHIRE
CRAFT BREWERS
2008/09

T0347000

COMPILED BY

GLOUCESTERSHIRE
CRAFT BREWERS
2008/09

First published 2008

The History Press Ltd
The Mill, Brimscombe Port
Stroud, Gloucestershire, GL5 2QG
www.thehistorypress.co.uk

British Library Cataloguing in Publication Data.
A catalogue record for this book is available from the British Library.

ISBN 978 0 7524 4783 4

Typesetting and origination by The History Press Ltd.
Printed in Great Britain

Contents

Martin Herbert promoting the Gloucestershire Craft Brewers at Tewkesbury Food and Drink Festival, 2007.

The Contributors

This guide was edited by Greg Pilley of Stroud Brewery with contributions from the Gloucestershire Craft Brewers and others.

Special thanks to Martyn Herbert, Gloucestershire CAMRA media officer, for compiling the 'ale trails' in this guide. Thanks also to Geoff Sandles, editor of *Tippler*, the Gloucestershire CAMRA newsletter, for his historical account of brewing in Gloucestershire, and to Tim Edgell for general support and not least for acting as the Gloucestershire Craft Brewers' contact address!

The Gloucestershire Craft Brewers is an association of eight microbreweries, which recognise that, despite their competition for the same market, there are benefits from working together to promote Gloucestershire beers and the breweries that produce them.

All royalties received from this publication will fund the future promotion of Gloucestershire real ales, and the Gloucestershire Ale Trail.

The Gloucestershire Craft Brewers are:

> Battledown Brewery
> Cotswold Spring Brewery
> Festival Brewery
> Nailsworth Brewery
> North Cotswold Brewery
> Severn Vale Brewing Company
> Stanway Brewery
> Stroud Brewery

ONE

The Gloucestershire Ale Trail

Hop harvesting in Herefordshire, 2007.

The Gloucestershire Ale Trail

The Gloucestershire Ale Trail is an initiative of the Gloucestershire Craft Brewers. Its aim is to strengthen the market for locally brewed beers by encouraging pubs to sell Gloucestershire beers and drinkers to drink them; in support of their local breweries and for the love of quality ale.

There are currently fifteen breweries in Gloucestershire which collectively brew over sixty different beers! Their greatest barrier is the steady loss of free-trading pubs, the majority being owned by pub management companies and a few large national breweries. This results in a lack of choice for beer drinkers, with many pubs offering a limited range of national brands.

The Gloucestershire Craft Brewers believe that the overall market for quality local beers can be improved if consumers and pubs have a greater interest and loyalty to local and Gloucestershire beers, and better information about where to buy them.

WHAT IS IT?
Simply, The Gloucestershire Ale Trail promotes those pubs and outlets where you are guaranteed to find a draught Gloucestershire beer.

This guide lists pubs in Gloucestershire that are committed to keeping Gloucestershire beers, and provides suggestions for 'ale trails' that may be taken by foot, bicycle or by public transport.

HOW DOES IT WORK?

The Gloucestershire Ale Trail will be monitored by you, the drinkers of Gloucestershire beers. If you have visited an outlet that has been listed in this book or on the Gloucestershire Ale Trail website and have been disappointed not to find a Gloucestershire beer, then contact any of the Gloucestershire Craft Brewers and let us know. If we receive repeated reports about that outlet we will remove them from ongoing promotional activity. Similarly, pubs that you know that always have a Gloucestershire beer available can be proposed for listing.

Stroud Brewery – the 'brewhouse'.

Greg mashing in at Stroud Brewery.

Racking beer into 9-gallon firkins at Stroud Brewery.

Greg Pilley of Stroud Brewery.

Map

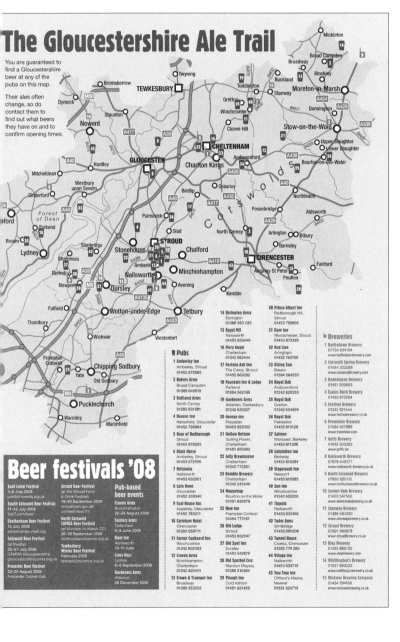

TWO

Brewing in Gloucestershire

A vintage Stroud Brewery truck.

A Potted History

Geoff Sandles

Just over thirty years ago the esteemed CAMRA Good Beer Guide described Gloucestershire as a 'poor county for real ale'. It seemed that everywhere you went in the county was a Whitbread pub. Tankard and Trophy Bitter were the beers that you were supposed to drink. The Whitbread Flowers brewery in Cheltenham produced their fair share of the gassy keg beer of the 1970s but one 'local' beer – West Country Pale Ale – survived throughout the decade. It was a fairly unremarkable beer of low strength but it had a loyal following. However, Whitbread in Cheltenham was not the only brewery in Gloucestershire in the mid-1970s. The Donnington Brewery, tucked away in a tranquil valley near Stow-on-the-Wold, was the epitome of a traditional country real ale brewery. Totally unspoilt by progress, Donnington Brewery owned seventeen pubs where their wonderful beers could be enjoyed in some of the most picturesque villages in the Cotswolds. If only Whitbread pubs could have been so good!

If I had been drinking 'local' beer twenty years earlier, in the 1950s, I would have been able to choose from Stroud Brewery 'Cotswold Beers' and Cheltenham Ales, both fiercely independent regional breweries with a proud heritage. Both these companies had grown by taking over – usually by mutual agreement – and closing smaller Gloucestershire breweries. Stroud Brewery, for example, had acquired Godsells of Salmon Springs and Cooks Tetbury Brewery. The market town brewers had fallen on hard times after the First World War, and their valuable pub estate ensured that the larger breweries had a guaranteed outlet for their beers. In late Victorian times there was an abundance of market town breweries throughout Gloucestershire – a real-ale drinker's idea of heaven! Two world wars with the resultant austerity meant that the reduction of brewing in Gloucestershire was inevitable.

The Stroud and Cheltenham Breweries amalgamated in 1958 to form West Country Breweries, and five years later Whitbread acquired the entire business. The legacy of West Country Ales remain in numerous colourful 'Best in the West' ceramic plaques inlaid into pub walls. The Cheltenham 'Flowers Brewery' closed in 1997, bringing to an end many years of brewing heritage in the town. The once-monopolistic Whitbread pub estate was also sold and leased, creating a new opportunity for a new wave of fledging Gloucestershire brewers. Uley Brewery was established in 1985, followed by Wickwar in 1990 and Freeminer in 1992. Brewing in Gloucestershire was again firmly back on the map.

In 2002 the Chancellor introduced a system of progressive beer duty, cutting the duty paid by small breweries. This has enabled the emergence of several new craft breweries, and it is now possible to drink a fantastic range of traditional beers produced by the new market-town brewers.

Opposite above: *Manual bottling at the old Stroud Brewery.*

Opposite below: *The old Stroud Brewery – the Fermenting Room.*

The old Stroud Brewery building in 1951.

THREE

The Gloucestershire Craft Brewers and Their Beers

BATTLEDOWN BREWERY
ROLAND ELLIOTT-BERRY
KEYNSHAM STREET
CHELTENHAM
GL52 6EJ

T: 01242 693409
M: 07734 834104
E: roland@battledownbrewery.com
www.battledownbrewery.com

In a move to revive the town's rich and illustrious brewing heritage, Battledown became the new brewery for Cheltenham three years ago, filling a gap left by the closure of the Whitbread Flowers Brewery eleven years ago.

Tucked into an old engineering works in a quiet little back-water close to the town's centre, Battledown is producing a small range of fine hand-crafted (and increasingly award-winning) ales for sale both into the trade and directly to the public.

In the years the brewery has been going, it has built up a gratifying local following, helped by its open-house policy, always welcoming visitors to come and see where and how the beers are produced, some of which are described here.

Saxon (3.8% ABV)
A golden pale ale, with a refreshing aroma and sharp but smooth taste, leaving a dry hoppy aftertaste which lingers on the palette.

Sunbeam (4.0% ABV)
California Common (aka American 'Steam Beer'). A gold and tasty ale brewed in the American Gold Rush way, using lager yeast and Northern Brewer hops.

Tipster (4.2% ABV)
Originally brewed for Cheltenham race weeks, but now a permanent fixture. A golden beer, the malts evident but giving way to the triple-hop addition to give a spicy and slightly citrus finish.

Brigand (4.7% ABV)
A rich, amber best bitter beer, with a fine malty aroma and taste and deeply satisfying full-bodied fruit and malt texture, leaving a well-rounded mellow aftertaste.

Cheltenham S.P.A. (5.2% ABV)
Special Pale Ale. A crisp and slightly fruity pale ale. Triple-hopped in the original India Pale Ale tradition.

COTSWOLD SPRING BREWERY
NIK MILO
COTSWOLD SPRING BREWERY
DODINGTON ASH
CHIPPING SODBURY
SOUTH GLOUCESTERSHIRE
BS37 6RX

T: 01454 323088
E: info@cotswoldbrewery.com
www.cotswoldbrewery.com

Cotswold Spring Brewery was established in the spring of 2005. They only use 100% finest malted barley, subtle blends of hops and pure Cotswold spring water. Their beers are fermented in traditional vessels using specialist strains of yeast and naturally conditioned in the cask. They contain NO artificial preservatives, flavourings or colourings. They aim to run a 'public' brewery, so drop in anytime and see what their brewer, Nik (the bear), is up to!

Olde English Rose (4.0% ABV)
Straw-like in colour, this excellent ale suggests every aspect of summer. With an initial dryness on the pallet and a hoppy finish, this brew is bursting with flavour.

Gloucestershire's Glory (4.1% ABV)
A golden beer with a distinctive citrus hop nose, mouth-filling malt and fruit, and a deep dry finish.

Codrington Codger (4.2% ABV)
A dry, crisp, amber, perfectly balanced beer with a mild hoppy finish.

Codrington Royal (4.5% ABV)
Ruby in colour and strong in multi-malt flavours. This well-balanced beer produces rich fruit flavours with a hint of spiciness.

Plus, it is a regular seasonal special.

FESTIVAL BREWERY
ANDY FORBES
UNIT 17 MALMESBURY ROAD
KINGSDITCH INDUSTRIAL ESTATE
CHELTENHAM
GLOUCESTERSHIRE
GL51 9PL

T: 01242 521444
E: info@festivalbrewery.co.uk

Festival Brewery is located on Cheltenham's Kingsditch Industrial Estate. The ten-barrel brewery is a hybrid of former plants from Stonehenge and Sharps brewery. The Festival Brewery name reflects the importance of Cheltenham as a venue for international festivals, and gives great scope for local-themed beers.

Festival Bitter (3.8 % ABV)
A well-balanced and refreshing beer with an appetising crisp, hoppy aftertaste. Copper in colour and made with German Northern Brewer hops for bittering and Styrian Golding and Willamette for aroma, giving a subtle fruity flavour.

Festival Gold (4.4% ABV)
Refreshing golden ale with a clear flavour that continues right through to the finish.

Festival Ruby (4.7% ABV)
A strong bitter, ruby-coloured with a rich, warming character.

NAILSWORTH BREWERY
JON KEMP
THE CROSS
BATH ROAD
NAILSWORTH
GL6 0HH

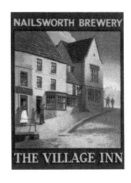

T: 01453 835715
M: 07878 448377
E: jonk@nailsworth-brewery.co.uk
www.nailsworth-brewery.co.uk

Opened in 2006, the Nailsworth Brewery and Village Inn pub combine to form Gloucestershire's only brew pub. The six-barrel plant sees a welcome return to brewing in Nailsworth after a drought lasting nearly 100 years. A craft brewery through and through, we use the time-honoured processes unchanged from the time of the original Nailsworth Brewery, and still not a computer in sight.

A brewing process which uses spring water (drawn from their own well), the finest of brewing malts (Marris Otter) and buckets of hops (ten varieties in all) from England and further afield ensures ales of quality, distinction and flavour.

Alestock (3.6% ABV)
More hoppy than a caffeine-fuelled bunny on a bouncy castle. The perfect summer ale. Originally brewed for Nailsworth's Nailstock music festival, it proved too popular for a 'one off' and so it has become our Summer special.

The Artist's Ale (3.9% ABV)
Light in colour, high on taste. A zingy, tangy, thirst-quenching bitter full of citrus flavours. Refreshingly moreish session beer.

The Mayor's Bitter (4.2% ABV)
A best bitter with wonderful malt textures, complemented by the long-lasting and heavenly taste of blackcurrants.

The Vicar's Stout (4.5% ABV)
Everything a traditional stout should be. Dark, rich, smoky, pleasantly bitter and very comforting.

The Town Crier (4.7% ABV)
A traditional premium ale full of rich and fruity flavours. One to be savoured rather than rushed.

NORTH COTSWOLD BREWERY
JON PILLING
DITCHFORD FARM
MORETON IN MARSH
GLOUCESTERSHIRE
GL56 9RD

**NORTH COTSWOLD
BREWERY**

T: 01608 663947
M: 07518 745851
E: mail@northcotswoldbrewery.co.uk
www.northcotswoldbrewery.co.uk

The North Cotswold Brewery came into new ownership in 2005. It is a ten-barrel plant brewing a range of regular and seasonal beers, totalling twenty-five different brews in all. The brewery has a shop and a visitor's centre where you can buy a large range of bottled beer, ciders and perrys. They also own the Happy Apple Cider Company and specialise in outside bars and farmers' markets.

Pig Brook (3.8% ABV)
A full-flavoured session beer. Goes well with food.

Hung-Drawn-N-Portered (5.0% ABV)
Strong black treacle porter with a balanced taste. An award-winner.

Ditchford Farm Ale (5.3% ABV)
A chestnut-coloured, traditional strong bitter.

Summer Solstice (4.5% ABV)
A cask lager brewed with German/Czech hops with a touch of spice.

Shag Weaver (4.5% ABV)
Pale, hoppy bitter made with New Zealand hops.

SEVERN VALE BREWING COMPANY
STEVE MCDONALD
SEVERN VALE BREWING COMPANY
LOWER KNAPP FARM
WOODEND LANE
CAM, DURSLEY
GL11 5HS

T: 01453 547550
M: 07971 640244
E: severnbrew@gmail.com
www.severnvalebrewing.co.uk

Established in 2005 in Cam, Severn Vale Brewing Co has won several awards for its ales, including a gold medal from SIBA (Society of Independent Brewers).

We brew a broad range of beers, from a 3.4% session ale to a strong stout. Output has gradually increased since start-up, and owner Steve McDonald still does all the work himself, although there are some weeks which don't have enough hours in them!

Adopted as Gloucester's local brewery, we work with Gloucester CAMRA at various events. Brewery visits can be arranged by appointment.

STOP PRESS: Severn Sins voted SIBA Supreme Champion Beer of Britain!

Session (3.4% ABV)
A low-gravity traditional bitter, brewed for those who like a couple of pints at lunchtime, or those in for a session!

Vale Ale (3.8% ABV)
Brewed from four different hop varieties to give a complex nose and flavour, this traditionally styled ale has a full-bodied malty character.

Dursley Steam Bitter (4.2% ABV)

Brewed to commemorate the 150th anniversary of the local branch line, and fondly remembered as the 'Dursley Donkey', this beer is our best-seller. Light and refreshing, with a soaring flowery hop nose and palate.

Severn Bells (4.3% ABV)

Wonderfully light and refreshing, this summer ale is available from May to September. Brewed with two types of aroma hop to give a zingy citrus flavour.

Severn Sins (5.2% ABV)

SIBA Supreme Champion Beer of Britain 2008!
Wonderfully dark and warming, this strong stout is full of chocolate and roast barley flavours, with subtle hops coming through in the finish.

STANWAY BREWERY
ALEX PENNYCOOK
STANWAY
CHELTENHAM
GLOUCESTERSHIRE
GL54 5PQ

T: 01386 584320
E: alex@stannybitter.f9.co.uk
www.stanwaybrewery.co.uk

Stanway Brewery was the original brewhouse for Stanway House, a sixteenth-century Jacobean manor house. The brewery is the only plant in the country still known to use wood-fired coppers.

Stanney Bitter (4.5% ABV)
A light, refreshing amber-coloured beer, dominated by hops in the aroma with a bitter taste and a hoppy, bitter finish.

Cotteswold Gold (3.9% ABV)
A refreshingly light summer ale with a delicate hop aroma. Cotteswold is the old name for the Cotswolds.

Lords-a-Leaping (4.5% ABV)
A dark, full-bodied beer with a strong, crystal malt character. This winter brew derives its name from the link with Stanway House and the traditional Christmas song.

Morris-a-Leaping (3.9% ABV)
A copper-coloured beer with a dry bitterness, finishing with a hoppy citrus aftertaste.

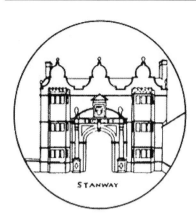

STROUD BREWERY

GREG PILLEY & IAN THORN (HEAD BREWER)
141 THRUPP LANE
THRUPP STROUD
GLOUCESTERSHIRE
GL5 2DQ

M: 07891 995878
E: greg@stroudbrewery.co.uk
www.stroudbrewery.co.uk

Stroud Brewery is a craft brewery producing premium, naturally conditioned beers using high-quality ingredients. They use whole hops and their malting barley is grown in the Cotswolds.

Stroud Brewery celebrates the things that make the 'Five Valleys' of the Stroud District special, and tries to share it with those a little further afield.

As well as running Stroud Brewery, Greg is a local food consultant dedicated to re-localising economies and sustainable production. To this end, Stroud Brewery has made the move to produce a range of organic beers. They have organic certification with the Soil Association and launched their first organic beer in the spring of 2008.

Tom Long (3.8% ABV)

An amber session beer with a spicy, citrus aroma. Overall SIBA Champion of the West of England and Wales 2008, and Silver in class at the National Championship 2008.

Stroud Organic Ale (4.0% ABV)

A fresh, hoppy golden organic ale. The first of Stroud Brewery's organic range of beers.

Teasel (4.2% ABV)

A classic best bitter, full-bodied, fruity and dry on the finish. Great with a meal.

Budding (4.5% ABV)
Champion Beer of Gloucestershire 2006. A pale ale with a grassy bitterness, sweet malt and luscious floral aroma.

Five Valleys (5.0% ABV)
A traditional chestnut-coloured, rich and fruity strong ale.

NOTE:
All the pubs listed in this guide guarantee that you will find
a Gloucestershire-brewed beer served at their premises.

FOUR

The Ale Trail Pubs

THE AMBERLEY INN
CULVER STREET
AMBERLEY
STROUD
GLOUCESTERSHIRE
GL5 5AF

T: 01453 872565
E: info@theamberley.co.uk
www.theamberley.co.uk

Opening times:
Mon – Sat: 11.00 – 23.00
Sun: 12.00 – 22.30

Nestled in the hidden heart of the Cotswolds, the elegant Amberley Inn looks over the renowned Five Valleys of Stroud. Situated close to the small town of Minchinhampton, it is quoted by some to be one of best examples of true Gloucestershire hospitality.

The Amberley Inn offers a picturesque setting. Many of its rooms offer views of the historic valley of Woodchester, home of the Orpheus Pavement dating back to AD 325. It appears that even the Romans appreciated the beauty of the Five Valleys.

The Amberley Inn.

The Bakers Arms.

THE BAKERS ARMS
BROAD CAMPDEN
GL55 6UR

T: 01386 840515

Opening times:
Summer: All day
Winter: Varies

This is a traditional Cotswold pub serving five real ales in a friendly atmosphere, with exposed Cotswold stone walls, beams, an inglenook fireplace, large car park and garden. Excellent Stanney Bitter and Donnington BB are permanent Gloucestershire beers on sale here. A Gloucestershire CAMRA award-winning pub. Good value, home-cooked meals available every day from November until March, and all day, every day, from April until October. Ingredients are sourced locally wherever possible.

THE BATHURST ARMS
NORTH CERNEY
CIRENCESTER
GLOUCESTERSHIRE
GL7 7BZ

T: 01285 831281
E: info@bathurstarms.com
www.bathurstarms.com

Opening times:
Mon – Sat: 12.00 – 15.00 and 18.00 – 23.00.
Sun: 19.00 – 22.30

Set in the picturesque village of North Cerney, right on the edge of the river Churn, the Bathurst Arms offers the intimacy of a traditional inn, combined with the high standards of food, wine and accommodation expected by a discerning traveller.

For those warm summer days and evenings, there is a pretty flower-filled garden running down to the river Churn. Whether it is for a one-night stop, a mid-week break, or a base for a longer stay from which you can explore the Cotswolds, the Bathurst Arms will ensure you have a visit to remember. There are six en-suite bedrooms, each individually and traditionally designed, one of which has a four-poster bed. All have tea- and coffee-making facilities. You can also wing-walk or go ballooning in the local area.

The Bathurst Arms.

THE BEACON INN
HARESFIELD
GLOUCESTER
GLOUCESTERSHIRE
GL10 3DX

T: 01452 728884
E: terry@thebeaconinn.co.uk
www.thebeaconinn.co.uk

Opening times:
Mon – Thurs: Lunchtime and evenings.
Fri – Sun: All day. See website for details.

The Beacon is a traditional village inn with character and high-quality facilities. Above all, you can be assured of a warm welcome and individual service.

Within easy reach of the motorway, yet surrounded by the rolling hills of the Cotswolds. The Beacon Inn is an ideal base for all – from a one-night stopover to a long break, in which you can explore the beautiful county of Gloucestershire.

The traditional bar, with its welcoming ambience, is stocked with a good range of beers, spirits and wines, as well as non-alcoholic drinks. And on those warm summer days and nights you are welcome to relax with your drinks and food on our recently extended patio.

The Beacon Inn.

THE BEAR OF RODBOROUGH HOTEL
RODBOROUGH COMMON
STROUD
GLOUCESTERSHIRE
GL5 5DE

T: 01453 878522
E: info@bearofrodborough.info
www.cotswold-inns-hotels.co.uk/bear

Opening times: 11.00 – 23.00

Nestling on the top of a steep hill, The Bear of Rodborough is situated in the historic south-west corner of the Cotswolds. This seventeenth-century former coaching inn has forty-six bedrooms in an area of outstanding natural beauty.

Enjoy fine traditional British ales in the Grizzly Bar. There is an extensive menu here if you wish to lunch or dine in a more relaxed atmosphere. The delightful Yorkstone terrace area, and the walled croquet lawn and gardens provide the perfect spot for relaxing with friends, or just catching the sun in the afternoon or on a warm summer's evening.

Every Easter weekend, the Bear hosts its own Real Ale Festival – this mouth-watering event will give you the chance to sample thirty local real ales, traditional ciders and English wines, all from Gloucestershire and the surrounding counties.

The Grizzly bar at The Bear.

THE BLACK HORSE
LITTLEWORTH
AMBERLEY
STROUD
GLOUCESTERSHIRE
GL5 5AL

T: 01453 872556
E: office@blackhorseamberley.co.uk
www.blackhorseamberley.co.uk

Opening times:
Daily: 12.00 – 23.00
Fri and Sat: 12.00 – 01.00

The Black Horse is everything one could possibly want of a village pub. Perched on the edge of Amberley, with one of the most stunning views in the Cotswolds, it has proudly retained its traditional pub values: a genuinely warm welcome, a selection of the finest real ales, good pub food and roaring fires.

With popular local ales such as Stroud Budding, featuring as permanent residents of the ale list, The Black Horse hosts a minimum of six real ales at any one time. Great pride and attention is taken in keeping and serving a really great pint, and, with that in mind, we look forward to you joining us for a beer!

The Black Horse.

The view from The Black Horse, Amberley.

THE BRITANNIA
COSSACK SQUARE
NAILSWORTH
GL6 0DG

T: 01453 832501
E: britannia@food-club.com
www.food-club.com

Opening times:
Mon – Thurs:	11.00 – 23.00
Fri and Sat:	11.00 – 00.00
Sun:	11.00 – 22.30

The Britannia, in the heart of Nailsworth, occupies a former manor house stretching the entire south side of Cossack Square. A vibrant town-centre establishment, it boasts an open-plan restaurant, snug bars and log fires, plus well-serviced gardens and plentiful parking. A great place for mid-morning coffee and cakes, or something from the extensive menu.

The Britannia.

CIRENCESTER & COATES

This page: Corinium Hotel, Cirencester.

Opposite above: Corinium Hotel, Cirencester.

Opposite above and below: The popular Tunnel House, Coates.

CAFÉ RENÉ
31 SOUTHGATE STREET
GLOUCESTER
GLOUCESTERSHIRE
GL1 1TP

Cafe Rene.

T: 01452 309340
E: caferene_gloucester@yahoo.co.uk
www.caferene.co.uk

Opening times:
Mon – Thurs: 12.00 – 00.00
Fri: 12.00 – 03.00
Sat: 11.00 – 03.00

With a friendly atmosphere inside and out, set amidst the historic surroundings of Gloucester, Café René is the place to be. Our venue entertains everything from candlelit dining to poker nights in the Cellar Bar, and rugby on the big screen to the best of Gloucester's live music.

We have freshly prepared quality food produced on the premises from 12.00 to 21.30 daily, with very pleasant dining in the restaurant and daily chef's specials. Our barbeques in the summer are legendary.

Whether you would like to eat, drink or just have a cup of fresh coffee, Café René is the place to be! Recommended by *The Rough Guide to England.*

Coal House Inn, Gloucester.

COAL HOUSE INN
GABB LANE
APPERLEY
GLOUCESTER
GLOUCESTERSHIRE
GL19 4DN

T: 01452 780211

Opening times:
Varies seasonally – call to confirm. Mid-October to mid-March, we are closed on Sunday evenings and Mondays.

This riverside pub has been a licensed house since at least the mid-eighteenth century, when it doubled as a coal wharf, with passing barges taking coal upstream. The interior comprises a bar which almost stretches the full extent of the property, with exposed beams and a tiled floor. Good quality, home-cooked meals are served up to 13.45 at lunchtime and 21.00 in the evenings. Stone steaks are a speciality. Outside, a patio overlooks the river Severn, making it a lovely spot to while away a summer evening. The pub has its own moorings and is on the Severn Way. (The approach road is liable to flooding in the winter.)

ELEGANT PROMENADES

Top: *The Promenade.*

Above left: *Cheltenham's Montpellier.*

Above right: *The Jolly Brewmaster, Cheltenham.*

Opposite above: *The Rotunda, Montpellier, Cheltenham.*

Opposite middle: *The Imperial Gardens, Cheltenham.*

Opposite below: *Montpellier in Cheltenham.*

CORINIUM HOTEL & RESTAURANT
12 GLOUCESTER STREET
CIRENCESTER
GL7 2DG

T: 01285 659711
E: info@coriniumhotel.co.uk
www.coriniumhotel.com

Opening times: 11.00 to 23.00

The delightful sixteenth-century Corinium Hotel & Restaurant offers fifteen en-suite bedrooms, bar, brasserie-style restaurant and attractive beer garden at the rear, which is popular in the summer. The cosy bar provides a very relaxing atmosphere and is full of character and Cotswold charm. Listed in CAMRA's *Good Beer Guide*, there are always three local real ales on offer, two of which rotate weekly. By popular demand, Laurie Lee Bitter from Uley Brewery is always available. The bar also offers a wide range of other beers, wines and spirits. All food is cooked to order using fresh ingredients sourced from local suppliers.

Corinium Hotel.

The Corner Cupboard.

THE CORNER CUPBOARD
88 GLOUCESTER STREET
WINCHCOMBE
CHELTENHAM
GLOUCESTERSHIRE
GL54 5LX

T: 01242 602303
E: sturgez@btconnect.com
www.cornercupboard.co.uk

Opening times:
Winter: 11.00 – 15.00 and 17.30 – 00.00
Summer: 11.00 – 00.00

The Old Corner Cupboard is found in the Cotswold town of Winchcombe, providing great real ales, fine wines and hearty home-cooked, traditional food. Run by local brothers Andrew and Stewart Sturge, along with Stewart's wife Judith, and a team of friendly local staff and our resident ghost.

We are lucky to have a separate traditional cellar to keep all our real ales at the perfect temperature. Belonging to the Gloucestershire Ale Trail guarantees you a fine pint of local beer; in addition to these we often feature beers from surrounding counties so we are trying to do our 'green bit'. In the summer you will be able to try up five beers sitting in our garden, and we keep three real ales on in the winter to drink by the log burner.

CHANGING SEASONS

Top: *Ebrington Arms, Ebrington.*

Above: *Crown & Trumpet, Broadway.*

Opposite above: *Winter at Ebrington.*

Opposite below: *Ebrington interior.*

THE CRAVEN ARMS
BROCKHAMPTON
CHELTENHAM
GLOUCESTERSHIRE
GL54 5XQ

T: 01242 820410

Opening times: 12.00 – 15.00 and 18.00 – 23.00
Closed Sunday nights.

This attractive seventeenth-century pub is set in an area of outstanding natural beauty, tucked away in a hillside village with great views and walks. Inside, the bar and restaurant are separated by stone-mullioned windows, and it has a feel of an old-style traditional pub with wood burner and open fire.

It offers real ales, home-cooked traditional bar meals at lunchtime and in the evening, plus at night there is an additional menu of several specials. Come and try our grill stones, where you cook your own meat or fish on a hot rock. These are great fun and taste good too.

The Craven Arms.

The Crown & Trumpet.

THE CROWN & TRUMPET INN
CHURCH STREET
BROADWAY
WORCESTERSHIRE
WR12 7AE

T: 01386 853202
E: info@cotswoldholidays.co.uk
www.cotswoldholidays.co.uk

Opening times: 11.00 – 14.30 and 17.00 – 23.00

Situated behind the village green in Broadway is our traditional seventeenth-century inn, the Crown & Trumpet Inn. Built in Cotswold stone, it is CAMRA recommended and we have four exclusively brewed seasonal beers from the local Stanway Brewery and guest beers from Stroud and other Gloucestershire Craft Breweries. Just off the Cotswold Way, we also offer accommodation, with four rooms for mid-week and weekend breaks. The Crown & Trumpet also has wireless internet.

Serving lunch and dinner all through the week, using locally produced ingredients, we specialise in seasonal home-made dishes, including a Sunday roast with Cotswold beef and Tewkesbury mustard. We also host monthly jazz and blues evenings.

SUMMER DAYS

This page: *Enjoying Gloucestershre's finest.*

Opposite above: *Colourful beer garden, Ebrington.*

Opposite below: *Coal House Inn garden, Apperly.*

THE EBRINGTON ARMS
EBRINGTON
CHIPPING CAMPDEN
GLOUCESTERSHIRE
GL55 6NH

T: 01386 593223
E: info@theebringtonarms.co.uk
www.theebringtonarms.co.uk

Opening times:
Mon: Closed except Bank Holidays.
Tues – Sat: 2.00 – 15.00 and 18.00 – Close
Sun: 12.00 – 22.30

Whether you seek absolute escapism, great company or some of the best locally sourced, home-cooked cuisine, The Ebrington Arms offers it all and much more, in one of the most serene settings in the Cotswolds.

Located in the unspoilt village of Ebrington (2 miles to Chipping Campden and Hidcote Gardens) this seventeenth-century inn offers a wide range of real ales and fine wines to be enjoyed in front of our roaring open fires. Recently rated four-out-of-five by CAMRA, we have three four-star en-suite rooms available on a bed & breakfast basis, a large beer garden and car park. A great base for walking and exploring the Cotswolds year-round.

Ebrington Arms interior.

Egypt Mill entrance.

EGYPT MILL
STATION ROAD
NAILSWORTH
GLOUCESTERSHIRE
GL6 0AE

T: 01453 833449
E: reception@egyptmill.com
www.egyptmill.com

Opening times:
Daily: 07.00 – 23.00

Situated on the banks of the river Frome with its two old waterwheels, Egypt Mill enjoys a unique setting, just a couple of minutes' walk from Nailsworth. Open all day for coffees and drinks, with a light lunch and full menu available at lunch-time, there is nowhere better to spend a leisurely afternoon. A full dinner menu is served every night and our large function suite is available for private parties. With twenty-eight great bedrooms, there is no need to leave!

OUT AND ABOUT IN THE COUNTRYSIDE

Above: *Swans enjoy the weather at Slimbridge Wildlife and Wetlands Trust, 2008.*

Opposite above: *Looking across the river Severn from Arlingham, a boatyard's colours compliment the surrounding environment.*

Opposite below, left: *May Hill, 2007.*

Opposite below, right: *A snowy morning in Frampton-on-Severn, 2008.*

THE FIERY ANGEL
83 HEWLETT ROAD
CHELTENHAM
GLOUCESTERSHIRE
GL52 6AJ

T: 01242 582444
E: fieryangel@foxmile.co.uk

Opening times:
Mon – Thurs: 17.00 – 23.00
Fri: 15.00 – 01.00
Sat and Sun: 12.00 – 00.00

Upon entering the Fiery Angel, you are welcomed with a warm and friendly atmosphere, with calm lighting and relaxing music. This modern bar and grill offers good value, homemade food, nurtured local ales and wine to suit all tastes. The décor is romantic with candles on every table and open fireplaces to create this charming environment.

The pub hosts a number of popular events, including a poker night, a fun quiz, seasonal activities and an open microphone night on Fridays, which is now one of the most exciting attractions in Cheltenham.

Left: *The Fiery Angel, Cheltenham.*

Right: *Foston's Ash Inn.*

THE FOSTON'S ASH INN
SLAD ROAD
THE CAMP
STROUD
GLOUCESTERSHIRE
GL6 7ES

T: 01452 863262
E: fostons-ash@food-club.com
www.food-club.com

Opening times:
Mon – Sat: 11.00 – 23.00
Sundays: 11.00 – 22.30

Set on the Cheltenham Road at the end of the Slad Valley, this really is *Cider with Rosie* country. With easy access from Cheltenham, Gloucester, Cirencester and Stroud, the Fostons Ash is a great drive-to destination and meeting place for friends. Lots of traditional features plus comfortable, contemporary furniture make for a stylish mix that updates the English country pub. This Grade II-listed, Cotswold-stone inn is named after a former turnpike keeper and is worth going the extra mile for, into the heart of the Cotswold Hills.

Retaining the original purpose-built cellar, the ales are particularly fine and Foston's Ash is proud to be part of the Gloucestershire Ale Trail, also situated close to the Cotswold Way. It is a must for roaming beer aficionados.

Foston's Ash is comfortable in every season, with long winter nights spent by the open log fires and summer days spent dining alfresco on the terrace or in the gardens. It offers areas for children, water bowls for the family pet and great food from our head chef, Mihai Sukosd, and his team.

A WARM WELCOME

Top: *New Inn, near Frampton Cotterel.*

Above: *The Rising Sun, Bream.*

Opposite: *Rising Sun sign.*

The Fountain Inn.

Gardener's Arms.

THE FOUNTAIN INN AND LODGE
FOUNTAIN WAY
PARKEND
GLOUCESTERSHIRE
GL15 4JD

T: 01594 562189
E: thefountaininn@aol.com
www.thefountaininnandlodge.com

Opening times:

Mon – Fri:	12.00 – 14.30 and 18.00 – 23.00
Sat:	12.00 – 23.00
Sun:	12.00 – 15.00 and 19.00 – 22.30

The Fountain Inn and Lodge is found in the delightful village of Parkend, set right in the heart of the Royal Forest of Dean, and is located within the boundaries of the Cannop Valley Nature Reserve.

Relax and enjoy a drink in our comfortable bar with its open fire and wonderfully cosy atmosphere. Choose from the extensive menu of traditional country fayre, much of which is created using local produce.

THE GARDENER'S ARMS
BECKFORD ROAD
ALDERTON
TEWKESBURY
GLOUCESTERSHIRE
GL20 8NL

T: 01242 620257
E: gardeners1@btconnect.com
www.gardenersarms.biz

Opening times: Vary between summer and winter.
Mon – Thurs: 12.00 – 14.30 and 18.00 – 23.00
Fri: 12.00 – 14.30 and 18.00 – 00.00
Sat: 12.00 – 15.00 and 18.00 – 23.00
Sun: 12.00 – 15.00 and 18.00 – 22.30

The Gardener's Arms is a sixteenth-century thatched country pub and restaurant in Alderton, a quiet village just north of Cheltenham in the heart of the Gloucestershire Cotswolds. A friendly, family-run free house where you'll find great food and a warm welcome from our staff.

We serve locally sourced, home-cooked food seven days a week, including seasonal produce such as asparagus and strawberries, with chef's specials which include fresh fish and game. We can also cater for specific allergies and are featured in several guides including the *Good Beer Guide* and *Good Pub Food Guide* to name but two. We run two Real Ale Festivals a year – on Spring Bank Holiday and on Boxing Day for one week – and have achieved the Cask-Marque award for the past five years, by consistently achieving a high standard of beer in terms of clarity, temperature, taste and aroma. We like to support as many microbreweries as possible, both local and national, and as such we change our ales regularly.

PUB EXTERIORS

Above: *The Old Spot., CAMRA Pub of the Year 2008.*

Opposite above: *The George at Frocester.*

Opposite centre: *The Saluation Inn.*

Opposite below: *The Salmon Inn.*

THE GEORGE INN
PETER STREET
FROCESTER
GLOUCESTERSHIRE
GL10 3TQ

T: 01453 822302
E: info@georgeinn.co.uk
www.georgeinn.co.uk

Opening times:
Mon – Thurs: 11.30 - 15.00 and 17.00 - 23.00
Fri – Sun: 11.30 – 23.00

Michael and Libby Reynolds welcome you to the George Inn at Frocester. The George Inn is a traditional eighteenth-century coaching inn, offering a fine selection of real ales and fine wines. Our food is all freshly prepared using local produce. The popular Sunday carvery is served from 12.30 to 20.30. Accommodation comprises of large en-suite bedrooms, some of which are family rooms. We have an AA three-star rating. Our function room is suitable for parties of up to eighty people. Afternoons and warm evenings can be spent in the courtyard garden with views to the Cotswolds and the village cricket green.

The
George Inn.

The Hollow Bottom.

THE HOLLOW BOTTOM
GUITING POWER
CHELTENHAM
GLOUCESTERSHIRE
GL54 5UX

T: 01451 850392
E: hello@hollowbottom.com
www.hollowbottom.com

Opening times: 9.00 – 00.30

A full range of beverages are available, from morning coffee and afternoon tea to a wide range of beers. Our ale list includes favourites like our own Hollow Bottom Best Bitter (brewed by Hall & Woodhouse) and London Pride, along with a regularly changing Gloucestershire ale from one of our local craft brewers such as Stroud, North Cotswold and Stanway.

Many years ago in our pub, customers had a whistle baked into the rim or handle of their ceramic cups. When they needed a refill, they would simply whistle to get some service. 'Wet your whistle' is the phrase inspired by this practice. However, we now use high-quality glassware!

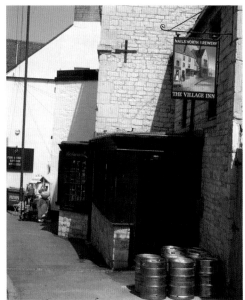

AROUND NAILSWORTH

Above: *The Village Inn.*

Opposite above: *Egypt Mill garden.*

Opposite below: *The Britannia.*

The Jolly Brewmaster.

THE JOLLY BREWMASTER
JOLLY BREWMASTER
39 PAINSWICK ROAD
CHELTENHAM
GLOUCESTERSHIRE
GL50 2EZ

T: 01242 772261

Opening Times: 12.00 – 23.00

Located on Painswick Road, the Jolly Brewmaster, or 'The Brew' as it is affectionately known, is a tucked-away gem. With a broad range of clientele from students to old locals, the atmosphere is always welcoming, laid-back and friendly.

With an unusual horseshoe-shaped bar, there are six real-ale hand-pumps which are constantly changing. It was the Cheltenham CAMRA Pub of the Year 2008. The Jolly Brewmaster garden is usually the biggest surprise for first-timers, much larger than one would expect, with rustic wooden tables and benches and an annual cider festival in July.

THE KEMBLE BREWERY
27 FAIRVIEW STREET
CHELTENHAM
GLOUCESTERSHIRE
GL52 2JF

T: 01242 243446

Opening times:
Mon – Thurs: 11.00 – 23.00
Fri and Sat: 11.00 – 00.00
Sun: 11.00 – 23.00

The Kemble Brewery – 'not just a pub but a way of life'.

Cheltenham's hidden oasis for the discerning real-ale drinker has six hand-pumps constantly changing, with local brews making every visit a new tasting experience.

You'll find us in the back streets of Fairview, easily mistaken for a private house – but don't be fooled. Once inside, it becomes a busy but quirky local, catering for all walks of life. Food is served daily, with the week culminating in a fabulous Sunday lunch.

The Kemble Brewery, Cheltenham.

MINCHINHAMPTON COMMON

Top: *The Old Lodge.*

Above left and right: *Signs on the Common.*

Opposite: *The Black Horse, Amberley by night.*

THE MOUSETRAP INN
LANSDOWNE
BOURTON ON THE WATER
CHELTENHAM
GLOUCESTERSHIRE
GL54 2AR

T: 01451 820579
E: thebatesies@gmail.com
www.mousetrap-inn.co.uk

Opening times: 11.30 – 23.00

This attractive, friendly, Cotswold-stone pub serves well-kept local beers, one of which is brewed especially for The Mousetrap by a well-known local brewer. We also serve good value, home-cooked meals. Situated in the quieter Lansdowne part of Bourton, it is popular with the local community and has ten en-suite rooms for visitors. A traditional family-run free house, complete with feature fireplace, The Moustrap offers a welcoming atmosphere. At the front of the pub a patio area with tables and hanging baskets provides a sheltered suntrap in the summer.

The Mousetrap.

THE NEW INN
50 BADMINTON ROAD
MAYS HILL
NEAR FRAMPTON COTTEREL
BRISTOL
SOUTH GLOUCESTERSHIRE
BS36 2NT

T: 01454 773161
E: dallyinns@aol.com

Opening times:
Mon – Sat: 11.45 – 14.30 and 18.00 – 23.00
Sun: 12.00 – 22.00

Three guest ales available, which are changed two to three times a week. There is a CAMRA member discount on Sunday and Monday evenings. Enjoy real beer and real food in a real pub!

The New Inn.

PAINSWICK AND THE CAMP

Top: *Foston's Ash Inn.*

Above left and right: *The famous Painswick yew trees.*

Opposite above: *The Royal Oak Inn, Painswick.*

Opposite below: *Lych Gate, Painswick.*

The Old Lodge.

THE OLD LODGE
MINCHINHAMPTON COMMON
STROUD
GLOUCESTERSHIRE
GL6 9AQ

T: 01453 832047
E: old-lodge@food-club.com
www.food-club.com

Opening times:
Mon – Sat: 11.00 – 23.00
Sun: 11.00 – 22.30

In 1213, after the Norman Conquest, the wooded land we now know as Minchinhampton Common was confiscated and given to l'Abbaye aux Dames in Caen. Some 800 years later, Christophe (a Norman himself) and business partner Nick continue to add to this fascinating Anglo-French story. The Old Lodge itself dates back some 400 years and is reportedly a former hunting lodge of Henry VIII.

The Lodge has magnificent views and an envied position at the centre of the common, with its free-ranging cattle, and in the middle of Minchinhampton golf course. The stunning restaurant has floor-to-ceiling windows that look directly onto the common, and the professional yet relaxed service is delivered by David Almeida and his team.

THE OLD SPOT INN
HILL ROAD
DURSLEY
GLOUCESTERSHIRE
GL11 4JQ

T: 01453 542870
E: steveoldspot@hotmail.co.uk
www.oldspotinn.co.uk

Opening times:
Mon – Sat: 11.00 – 11.00
Sun: 12.00 – 11.00

This convivial local is CAMRA's National Pub of the Year 2008, and is described by landlord Steve Herbert as 'a pub of a thousand locals'. On the Cotswold Way and opposite a free car park, The Old Spot Inn is friendly, deeply traditional and one of the must-visits of the county.

There are normally at least eight guest real ales, mainly from microbreweries, a good selection of fine wines and a famous whisky collection, served in five separate drinking areas.

The wholesome menu boasts a selection of home-cooked meals and light snacks, available 12.00 – 20.00 on weekdays and 12.00 – 15.00 at weekends.

The Old Spot Inn.

AROUND WINCHCOMBE

Top: *The Gardener's Arms, Alderton.*

Above: *Hollow Bottom, Guiting Power.*

Opposite above: *The Sun Inn, Winchcombe.*

Opposite below: *The Royal Oak, Gretton.*

THE OLD SPOTTED COW
MARSTON MEYSEY
WILTSHIRE
SN6 6LQ

T: 01285 810264
E: anna@theoldspottedcow.co.uk
www.theoldspottedcow.co.uk

Opening times:
Tues-Fri: 12.00 – 14.30 and 17.30 – 23.00
Sat and Sun: 12.00 – 23.00

The Old Spotted Cow is on the outskirts of pretty Marston Meysey. The pub is set well back from the road with lovely views over the surrounding farmland, making it gloriously tranquil. Almost 200-years old, the Cow retains much of the character and ambience that make Cotswold pubs special. Open log fires at each end of the bar make winter visits a cosy prospect, and in summer the garden is charming. The staff are justifiably proud of their real ales, and good local food is a real emphasis here. Well worth a detour!

The Old Spotted Cow.

THE PLOUGH INN
COLD ASTON
GLOUCESTERSHIRE
GL54 3BN

The Plough Inn.

T: 01451 821459
E: info@theploughcoldaston.com
www.theploughcoldaston.com

Opening times:
Tues – Sun: 12.00 – 14.30 and 18.30 – 23.00

The Plough is a Grade II-listed, seventeenth-century inn, located in the peaceful and award-winning Cotswold village of Cold Aston. This quintessential British pub of immense charm began 2007 with a sympathetic refurbishment whilst retaining the original period features: low ceilings with oak beams, inglenook fireplace and flagstone floor.

Managers Karl Smith and Pip Baston, together with the owners and a team of friendly and efficient helpers, are committed to serving interesting food and beverages at affordable prices, and strive for the highest standards in all aspects of innkeeping.

A COTSWOLD MISCELLANY

Top: *The bar at the Craven Arms.*

Above: *The Plough Inn.*

Opposite above: *The Royal Oak, Andoversford.*

Opposite below: *The Mousetrap, Bourton-on-the-Water.*

The Prince Albert.

THE PRINCE ALBERT INN
THE BUTTS
RODBOROUGH HILL
STROUD
GLOUCESTERSHIRE
GL5 3SS

T: 01453 755600
www.princealbertstroud.co.uk

Opening times:
Mon – Sat: 17.00 – 00.00
Sun: 17.00 – 00.00

Situated on the edge of Rodborough, the Prince Albert is a friendly pub serving the community, visitors and the many walkers who come to the area. Excellent Sunday lunches are followed by film matinees – see the website for programme. Entertainment includes open mic sessions on Thursdays and bands on Saturdays. Board games are available, with crib and backgammon proving very popular, and there is wi-fi internet access and a public computer. It has a covered smoking area on the patio with table football and chimineas, and the pub is child- and dog-friendly. The bar has four hand-pulls with the local Stroud Brewery always represented, and a fine selection of ciders. Parking is limited, but it is well worth the walk to relax by the log fire on a comfy sofa!

THE RAM INN
STATION ROAD
WOODCHESTER
STROUD
GLOUCESTERSHIRE
GL5 5EQ

T: 01453 873329
E: jewantsum@aol.com

Opening times: 11.00 – 23.00

The pub celebrated its 400th birthday in 2001 and is located in superb walking country close to Woodchester Mansion. It offers three ever-changing guest ales. An Irish beer festival coincides with the National Hunt Festival at Cheltenham in March, and an anti-Beaujolais event promotes English beer and food. Good-value food is served in a separate restaurant area. A new extension has added a lounge area, wheelchair access and a new toilet block, and the pub is dog-friendly. The pub is a regular venue for the Stroud Morris Men.

The Ram Inn.

The Red Lion.

THE RED LION
THE CROSS
ARLINGHAM
GLOUCESTERSHIRE
GL2 7JH

T: 01452 740700
E: redlionarlingham@hotmail.co.uk
www.redlionarlingham.co.uk

Opening times:
Open lunchtimes and evenings.
Closed Mondays, except bank holidays. Phone to confirm.

13 miles south of Gloucester is a great bend in the river Severn, forming a peninsula on the eastern bank. On the western end of this peninsula lies the small village of Arlingham. The centre of the village is built around The Cross and situated here is the Red Lion, a large village pub, partly dating from the sixteenth century, which offers accommodation, a friendly atmosphere, a warm welcome and excellent food. The Red Lion has a skittle alley available for teams needing an alley or simply a neutral alley. It can also be used as a function room for parties, wedding receptions etc., and can be hired free of charge.

THE RISING SUN
HIGH STREET
BREAM
GLOUCESTERSHIRE
GL15 6JF

T: 01594 564555
E: jonjo_risingsun@msn.com
www.therisingsunbream.co.uk

Opening times:
Mon – Fri:	12.00 – 14.30 and 18.30 – 23.00
Sat:	12.00 – 23.00
Sun:	12.00 – 14.30 and 19.00 – 22.30

The pub stands at the top of the High Street opposite the war memorial. The pub was first recorded as an inn in 1787 and the earliest part of the building dates from 1729. Since that time the pub has been extended. It was kept by various members of the Morse family until it became an Arnold Perrett pub, before being taken over by the Cheltenham Original Brewery in 1937. For a short period during the 1990s it was completely gutted, extended and became the Village Inn. The Rising Sun is now a free house with a range of regular local ales. It has twice been named 'Forest of Dean Pub of the Year' by the Forest branch of CAMRA.

The Rising Sun.

THE ROYAL OAK
GLOUCESTER ROAD
ANDOVERSFORD
GLOUCESTERSHIRE
GL54 4EH

T: 01242 820335

Opening times:
Mon – Sun: 11.00 – 15.00 and 17.00 – 23.00

The Royal Oak Inn is situated on the banks of the river Coln, in the heart of the Cotswolds. Placed just off the Cotswold Way, it makes an ideal starting and finishing point for countryside walks. The bar provides a warm and friendly atmosphere in which to enjoy a well-kept pint of locally brewed ale, while diners can relax in the galleried restaurant and choose from a wide variety of meals, cooked from fresh using locally sourced produce.

The Royal Oak, Andoversford.

THE ROYAL OAK
GRETTON ROAD
GRETTON
GL54 5EP

T: 01242 604999

Opening times:
Mon – Sat: 12.00 – 15.30 and 18.00 – 23.30
Sun: 12.00 – 16.00 and 18.00 – 23.00

Enjoy the friendly, if not eccentric, atmosphere of this lovely Cotswold pub. Serving great food, fine ales, and fine wines. Try the homemade steak pie, the sea bass or the salmon, or even our crab salad. Great for your love life! Enjoy the views or have a game of tennis in our garden. Handy for the GWR railway station at Winchcombe.

The Royal Oak, Gretton.

The Royal Oak, Painswick.

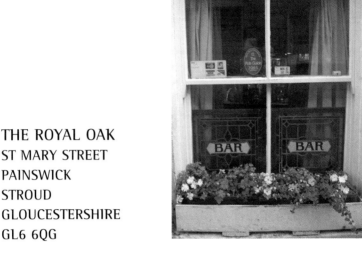

THE ROYAL OAK
ST MARY STREET
PAINSWICK
STROUD
GLOUCESTERSHIRE
GL6 6QG

T: 01452 813129
E: royaloak@btconnect.com

Opening times:
Daily: 11.00 – 15.00 and 18.00 – 23.00

The Royal Oak in Painswick is a sixteenth-century pub-restaurant, nestled in the heart of this small, most quintessential Cotswold wool town near Stroud and Gloucester on the route of the Cotswold Way.

Family-owned and -run for the first time in nearly ten years, we specialise in creative and well-priced food, home-cooked using fresh and local produce, including traditional Sunday lunch. We serve local cask ales from Stroud Brewery, Cotswold Premium Lager form the Cotswold Brewing Company and four cask and draught ciders from the west of England, plus a range of very good wines. A warm and friendly atmosphere welcomes children and adults alike. Outside is a large and sunny courtyard, which is safe for children. Local musicians play here often, and there is a quiz evening on the first Thursday of every month.

The Salmon.

THE SALMON
WANSWELL
BERKELEY
GLOUCESTERSHIRE
GL13 9SE

T: 01453 811306
E: grant.hendy@btconnect.com

Opening times:
Mon – Thurs: Lunchtime and evenings.
Fri – Sun: All day.

An oak-beamed village pub with a few nooks and crannies, bare floorboards, dartboard, fruit machine, touch-screen games and crib/domino facilities. A large section of the pub is given over to diners, and children are always welcome. The front garden, with slides and swings, also doubles up as the village green.

THE SALUTATION INN
HAM GREEN
BERKELEY
GLOUCESTERSHIRE
GL13 9QH

T: 01453 810284

Opening times:
Mon: 17.00 – 23.00
Tue – Fri: 12.00 – 14.00 and 17.00 – 23.00
Sat and Sun: 12.00 – 23.00

The Salutation Inn is an old, unspoilt pub situated in the peaceful village of Ham (half a mile from Berkeley). It has a friendly, welcoming, cosy atmosphere, with a log burner in colder months. There is always a selection of four ales (mainly local), as well as a good choice of lagers, cider, wines, etc. Pub meals and snacks are available, and families are welcome.

With a large garden and car park, it is in an ideal location for walkers, with the Deer Park nearby. It is also popular with cyclists. The skittle alley is available for parties, functions or meetings.

The Salutation Inn.

THE STAGECOACH INN
NEWPORT
BERKELEY
GLOUCESTERSHIRE
GL13 9PY

T: 01453 810385
E: info@stagecoachinn.co.uk
www.stagecoachinn.co.uk.

Opening times:
Mon – Sat: 11.00 – 15.00 and 17.30 – 23.00
Sunday: All day.

The Stagecoach Inn is a traditional, family-owned and -run free house. Like many rural pubs it has been forced by eco-nomical circumstances to branch out into food in order to survive. However, we believe that cask ale is the one unique selling point of pubs, and as such it remains the cornerstone of our business. We always stock two national brands of cask ale, and two Gloucestershire ales. The current selection can be seen on our website.

The Stagecoach Inn.

THE SUN INN
NORTH STREET
WINCHCOMBE
GLOUCESTERSHIRE
GL54 5LH

T: 01242 602256

Opening times:
Mon – Thurs: 11.00 – 15.00 and 18.00 – 00.00
Fri – Sun: 11.00 – 00.00

We are a friendly local pub with all the usual pub games, and we also host live music and karaoke. Newly refurbished with a beer garden and outside smoking facilities, we have a wide range of beers, lagers and ciders. A local real ale, Stanney, is our best-seller. All are welcome to come and have a drink in the warm and friendly atmosphere of The Sun Inn.

The Sun Inn.

THE TIPPUTS INN
BATH ROAD
NAILSWORTH
GLOUCESTERSHIRE
GL6 0QE

The Tipputs Inn.

T: 01453 832466
E: tipputs@food-club.com
www.food-club.com

Opening times:
Mon – Sat: 11.00 – 23.00
Sun: 11.00 – 22.30

The Tipputs is found at the head of the valley, south of Nailsworth at Tiltups End, so-named because heavily laden carts leaving Nailsworth for Bath would tilt up or loose their load, which was only safe after crossing the brow of the escarpment, hence 'Tilt-ups end'. The sight of the coaching inn must have been a great relief to those hauliers of times past.

Food is served all day in the friendly bar and lounges, and the galleried restaurant in the former stone barn is a great venue for lunch and dinner. Easily found on the Great Southern Road to Bath, its pleasant garden terraces and expansive parking make the Tipputs a popular choice.

THE TUDOR ARMS
SHEPHERDS PATCH
SLIMBRIDGE
GLOUCESTERSHIRE
GL2 7BP

T: 01453 890306
E: anything@thetudorarms.co.uk
www.thetudorarms.co.uk

Opening times: 11.00 – 23.00

The Tudor Arms is a large, family-operated free house beside the Gloucester–Sharpness Canal, and just half a mile from the world-famous Slimbridge Wildfowl and Wetlands Trust. The building dates from the eighteenth century, and was a licensed beer and cider house for the Irish navvies who dug the canal by hand. Today, it is a fully licensed premises, with two bars offering a range of cask ales – including a guest cask – and keg ales, stouts, lagers and ciders. There is a games room with pool tables and a skittle alley adjacent to the Canal Bar.

We offer accommodation and are proud to have been CAMRA's 'Gloucester Country Pub of the Year' in 2007.

Left: *The Tudor Arms.*

Opposite: *The Tunnel House.*

THE TUNNEL HOUSE INN AND BARN
TARLTON ROAD
COATES
CIRENCESTER
GLOUCESTERSHIRE
GL7 6PW

T: 01285 770280
E: bookings@tunnelhouse.com
www.tunnelhouse.com

Opening times:
Mon – Thurs: 11.30 – 15.30 and 18.00 – 23.00
Fri – Sun: All day.

A prime example of a traditional Cotswold pub, set in an idyllic location, the Tunnel House Inn welcomes everyone. With plenty of space inside and out, families, children and dogs are all welcomed equally. We have traditional pub food at sensible prices, and, of course, local real ale. We also have a private barn for parties. Please come and visit, whether to sit by a cosy fire in the winter or outside on a Cotswold summer's day.

THE VILLAGE INN
THE CROSS
BATH ROAD
NAILSWORTH
GLOUCESTER
GL6 0AH

T: 01453 835715
E: jonk@nailsworth-brewery.co.uk
www.nailsworth-brewery.co.uk

The Village Inn sign.

Opening times:
Mon – Weds: 11.00 – 23.00
Thurs – Sat: 11.00 – 00.00
Sun: 12.30 – 10.30
Kitchen closed on Mondays

Nailsworth's Village Inn is a place to relax, unwind and enjoy the atmosphere of what is a truly traditional village pub, where everyone is made to feel welcome. Not only does the Village boast a superb, conversationally friendly layout and welcoming staff, it is also home to both the Nailsworth Brewery and Nailsworth Pie Company.

We always have six draft ales on tap (four brewed on the premises using water drawn from our own well) while our array of mouth-watering pies (some vegetarian) are made on the premises using the finest of fresh local ingredients.

We have a book club that meets on the first Monday of each month, a Sunday night quiz and on Thursday evenings we have amazing informal music sessions featuring a plethora of fine local talent. If you or your partner want to do something a little more challenging than reading the pub's newspapers, there is a selection of games available from behind the bar.

In 2008, CAMRA has voted us the best pub in the Stroud area and the Hash Harriers have voted us best pub in Gloucestershire. So take their lead, give us a visit and enjoy the craic at the Village Inn!

THE YEW TREE INN
50 MAY HILL
CLIFFORD'S MESNE
NEWENT
GLOUCESTERSHIRE
GL18 1JS

T: 01531 820719
E: cass@yewtreeinn.com
www.yewtreeinn.com

Opening times:
Daily: 12.00 – 14.30 and 18.00 – 23.00

A welcoming retreat on the slopes of Mayhill, formerly a cider house, the Yew Tree retains the old features and the atmosphere is relaxed and friendly. We have a minimum of two local real ales on at any one time, and a selection of artisan ciders and perrys. We hold an annual beer and cider festival in the spring.

The daily specials complement the seasonal menus, which include local favourites such as slow-roast belly of Old Spot pork with caramelised celeriac, and our famous rabbit and bacon pudding. Our free-range chickens provide eggs for the kitchen, and many of the herbs, salads, vegetables and fruit are home-grown.

Wines also feature prominently, as we import all of our own. They are available for purchase from our in-house shop, or can be enjoyed with a meal at a very reasonable price!

The Yew Tree Inn.

FIVE

Ale Trails

Strange statues, Cheltenham.

Ale Trails

The following trails link a selection of pubs listed in the Gloucestershire Ale Trail, starting and finishing at participating pubs. If you are using a pub car park, please check that you can leave your vehicle in the car park before you commence your walk. Alternatively, use the bus guide to travel by public transport to and from your walk. Most of the trails can be started at any of the pubs involved. Where shown, numbers in white circles are mileage points.

If you have any suggestions for a Gloucestershire Ale Trail walk or cycle, then please e-mail them to any Gloucestershire Craft Brewer, and we will post them on the Ale Trail website and may include them in next year's guide.

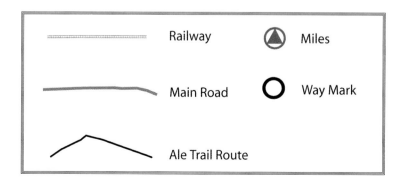

Trail 1
Winchcombe and Gretton

Starting from the rear of the Corner Cupboard (1) in Winchcombe, walk up Harveys Lane and follow the Wychavon Way up Langley Hill. Follow the path to the top of the hill and enjoy the superb views across the Cotswold escarpment. After passing the derelict Abbotleys Farm go through the gate and take the path straight on down to the track that takes you on to the Gretton–Winchcombe road. At the end of the track turn left and follow the road to the Royal Oak, Gretton (2). Enjoy a drink at the Oak before setting off back up the road to Winchcombe and into North Street, which takes you to the Sun Inn (3). From there continue on North Street to the end and turn right past the church back to the Corner Cupboard.

Winchcombe can be reached on the 606 Castleways service from Cheltenham Royal Well bus station.

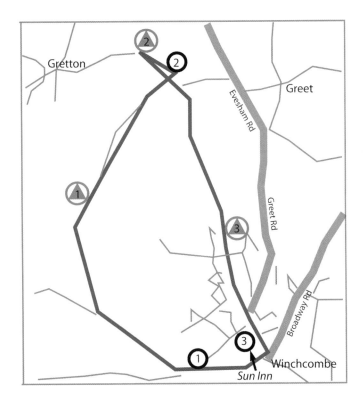

Trail 2
Bream and Parkend

Commencing at the Rising Sun in Bream (1) walk on the road towards Parkend, and after a pleasant stroll down the hill you arrive at the Fountain Inn and Lodge (2) near the Forest of Dean railway. From there walk along the road to Whitecroft before turning right back to Bream up the hill, which will build up your thirst for when you return to the Rising Sun.

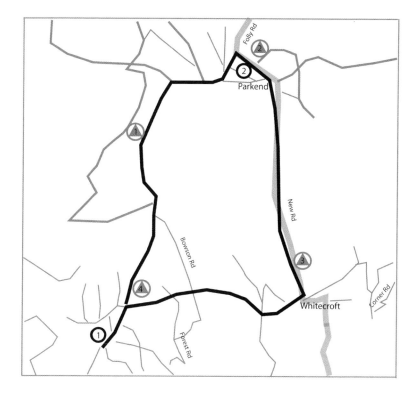

Trail 3
Bourton and Cold Aston

Start in Bourton and walk along the banks of the river to the main road, turn left and then right towards Cheltenham. Take the first left and follow the lane through to the village of Cold Aston. The Plough Inn is in the centre of the village on the left-hand side. After a refreshing drink, retrace your footsteps and visit the Mousetrap on the main Lansdown road back into Bourton.

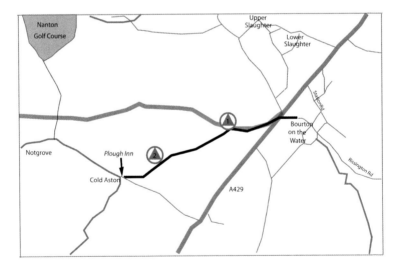

Trail 4
Nailsworth, Minchinhampton, Amberley and Wooodchester

Starting out from Nailsworth car park, cross the A46 and turn left along Watledge Road. Turn right up the footpath to Minchinhampton Common, and walk across the common where you can call in the Old Lodge (2) on the way towards Amberley and the Black Horse (3) on Culver Hill. Then walk round the corner to the Amberley Inn (4) before dropping drop down Culver Hill to Woodchester, cross the A46 and walk up Station Road to the Ram Inn (5). Walk back down the disused railway line into Nailsworth, where you can visit Egypt Mill (6) and the Village Inn (1), brewtap of the Nailsworth Brewery.

There are several buses serving Nailsworth from across the county.

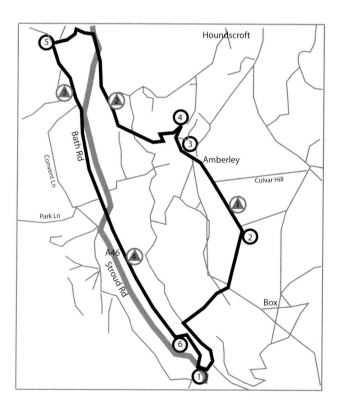

Trail 5
Broad Camden and Ebrington

Start from the Bakers Arms (1) and walk into Chipping Camden. Turn right and walk up the High Street before turning right into Church Street and then into Station Road. After going over the level crossing, take the next right at the top of hill into Ebrington, and then right again to the Ebrington Arms (2). Leaving the Ebrington Arms, continue on the road and take a right turn back to Chipping Camden, to return to the Bakers Arms.

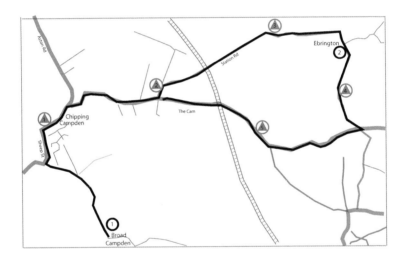

Trail 6
Rodborough

Starting from the Prince Albert (1) walk across the common to the Bear (2) and return with a walk around the common. You can join this route with Walk 4 to finish in Nailsworth, which has good transport links with Stroud.

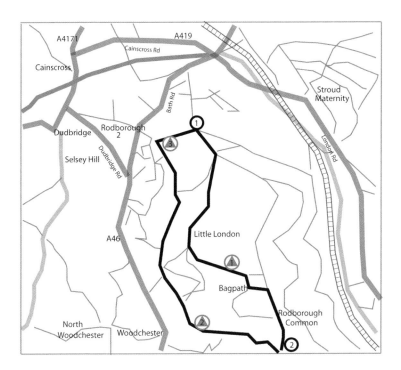

Trail 7
Andoversford and Brockhampton

Leave the Royal Oak (1) and turn right then first left along Station Road. Take the first footpath on the right which crosses the A40 and continues to Syreford. Continue on the footpath to Sevenhampton then turn right by the church and cross the stream. Take the track into Brockhampton and turn left at the end, and left again to the Craven Arms (2). For the return journey you can take the road back to Syreford or, when you leave the Craven, turn left and take the footpath to Sevenhampton church.

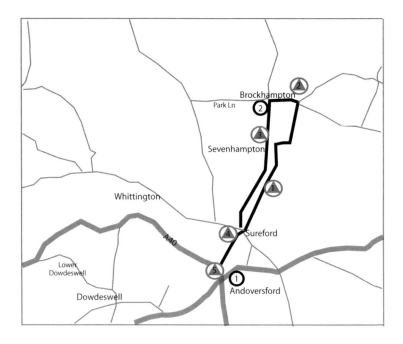

Trail 8
Bus and walk to Cliffords Mesne

Take the 32 bus from Gloucester or Newent to Kilcot Cross (stop after the Kilcot Inn). Walk to the crossroads and turn down the road to Aston Ingham. Follow the road for just over 2 miles, and as you reach Cliffords Mesne take the first right down the hill, and then right and right again to the Yew Tree (1). Alternatively, as you go through Aston Ingham, take the track to the left at the start of the long right-hand bend and follow the footpath over the hill, which brings you to the road just above the pub. For the return journey, walk down from the pub and turn left and stay on the bottom road, which leads straight back into Newent, where you can catch a 32 or 132 bus back to Gloucester every half hour.

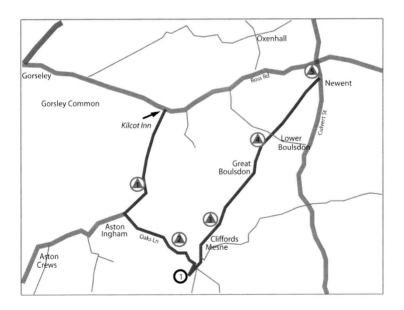

Trail 9
Cheltenham town centre

Using the map below you can choose your walk around Cheltenham, calling at the Jolly Brewmaster (1), the Kemble Brewery Inn (2) and the Fiery Angel (3).

There is a car park just off the Bath Road near the Jolly Brewmaster.

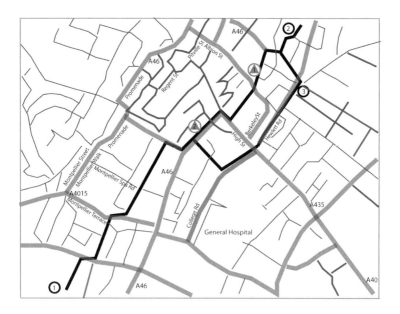

Trail 10
Berkeley area

Starting from the Salmon (1) at Wanswell, walk into Berkeley and turn left past the castle. Follow the road to the A38, turn right and you arrive at the Stagecoach Inn (2) at Newport. From here, if you walk back up the A38 a short distance, there is a footpath directly to Ham, but otherwise continue on the A38 southwards and turn right at Alkerton. Follow the lane through to Ham and the Salutation (3). From Ham continue back into Berkeley and back out on the road to Wanswell.

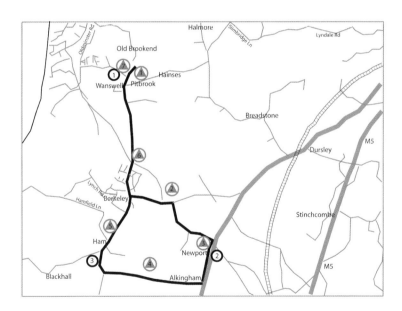

Trail 11
Poulton and Marston Meysey

Starting from the Falcon Inn (1) walk down the lane towards Down Ampney. After 2 miles turn left, then right, and follow the lane into Marston Meysey and visit the Old Spotted Cow (2). Continue through the village and follow the signs to Meysey Hampton. Turn right into the village, then left when you reach the main road, which takes you back to The Falcon Inn.

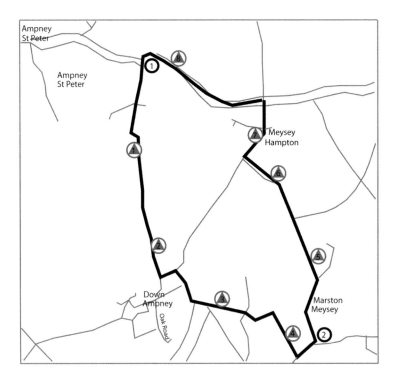

APPENDICES

Further Information

There is much shopping to be done around Cheltenham.

Events

A listing of key annual events.
Check www.glosaletrail.org.uk and the Gloucestershire
CAMRA website – www.gloucestershirecamra.org.uk – for up
to date events.

Event	Date	For More Details
Cirencester Beer Festival	24–27/04/08	www.cirencester-beerfestival.co.uk
Tewkesbury Food and Drink Festival	03–04/05/08	Katie Power, Festival Organiser on T: 01684 272249 or E: katiepower@ tewkesbury.gov.uk
Dursley Rugby Club	07/06/08	www.dursleyrfc.co.uk
Three Counties Show, Malvern	13–15/06/08	Gloucestershire Craft Brewers - Beer Tent
Cheltenham Food and Drink Festival	20–21/06/08	E: info@garden-events.com www.garden-events.com
Saul Canal Festival	04–06/06/08	www.junctionevents.org.uk
South Cotswold Beer Festival	11–12/07/08	www.bs37.com/beer
Cheltenham Beer Festival	12/07/08	www.samsfriends-chelt.org
Cotswold Beer Festival (Postlip)	25–27/07/08	CAMRA Gloucestershire www.gloucestershire camra.org.uk
Frocester Beer Festival	22–25/08/08	Frocester Cricket club
Stroud Beer Festival, Food and Drink Festival	19–20/09/08	www.stroudtown.gov.uk/ content/view/31/
North Cotswold CAMRA beer festival Moreton-in-Marsh C.C	26–28/09/09	www.northcotswoldcamra. org.uk
Tewkesbury Winter Beer Festival	February 2009	www.tewkesburycamra. org.uk

Pub Events

Pub	Date	Event
Gardeners Arms, Alderton	23–29/05/08	Summer Ale Festival
Craven Arms, Brockhampton	22–25/08/08	Beer Festival
Royal Oak, Andoversford	30/05/08– 01/06/08	
Farriers Arms, Todenham	06–08/06/08	
Boat Inn, Ashleworth	13–15/06/08	
Craven Arms, Brockhampton	22–25/08/08	
Cross Keys Beer Festival, Lydney	06–08/09/08	
Gardeners Arms, Alderton	26/12/08	Boxing Day Beer Festival
Bear of Rodborough	Easter 2009	Beer Festival

Bus Routes

No.	PUB	ADDRESS	POSTCODE	BUS SERVICES	DISTRICT
1	Amberley Inn	Amberley	GL5 5AF	28 OR 29 STROUD TO CIREN OR TETBURY	STROUD
2	Bakers Arms	Broad Campden	GL55 6UR	22 MORETON TO STRATFORD	COTSWOLD
3	Bathurst Arms	North Cerney	GL7 7BZ	51 CHELT TO CIREN	COTSWOLD
4	Beacon Inn	Haresfield	GL10 3DX	14 GLOS TO STROUD	GLOUCESTER
5	Bear of Rodborough	Rodborough Common	GL5 5DE	28 STROUD TO CIRENCESTER	STROUD
6	Black Horse	Littleworth	GL5 5AD	28 STROUD TO CIRENCESTER	STROUD
7	Britania	Nailsworth	GL6 0DG	40, 46, 93	STROUD
8	Café René	Gloucester	GL1 1TP		GLOUCESTER
9	Coal House Inn	Apperley	GL19 4DN	351 GLOS TO UPTON-ON SEVERN	GLOUCESTER
10	Corinium Hotel	Cirencester	GL7 2DG	51 CHELT TO CIREN	COTSWOLD
11	Corner Cupboard Inn	Winchcombe	GL54 5LX	606 CHELT TO WILLERSEY	COTSWOLD
12	Craven Arms	Brockhampton	GL54 5XQ	804 CHELT TO TEMPLE GUITING	COTSWOLD
13	Crown & Trumpet Inn	Broadway	WR12 7AE	606 CHELT TO WILLERSEY	COTSWOLD
14	Ebrington Arms	Ebrington	GL55 6NH	22 MORETON TO CHIPPING CAMPDEN	COTSWOLD
15	Egypt Mill	Nailsworth	GL6 0AE	40, 46, 93	STROUD
16	Fiery Angel	Cheltenham	GL52 6AJ		CHELTENHAM
17	Fostons Ash Inn	The Camp	GL6 7ES	256 GLOS TO	STROUD

No.	PUB	ADDRESS	POSTCODE	BUS SERVICES	DISTRICT
18	Fountain Inn and Lodge	Parkend	GL15 4JD	73 GLOS TO LYDNEY THEN 727	FOREST
19	Gardeners Arms	Alderton	GL20 8NL	526 WINCH TO TEWKESBURY	TEWKESBURY
20	George Inn	Frocester	GL10 3TQ	14 STROUD TO GLOS (LEONARD STANLEY)	STROUD
21	Hollow Bottom	Guiting Power	GL54 5UX	804 CHELT TO TEMPLE GUITING	COTSWOLD
22	Jolly Brewmaster	Cheltenham	GL50 2EZ	10 CHELTENHAM TO GLOUCESTER	CHELTENHAM
23	Kemble Brewery	Cheltenham	GL52 2JF		CHELTENHAM
24	Mousetrap	Bourton on the Water	GL54 2AR	801 CHELT TO MORETON	COTSWOLD
25	New Inn	Badminton Road, Mays Hill	BS36 2NT	X30 YATE TO BRISTOL GLOUCESTERSHIRE	SOUTH
26	Old Lodge	Minchinhampton Common	GL6 9AQ	28 OR 29 STROUD TO CIREN OR TETBURY	STROUD
27	Old Spot Inn	Dursley	GL11 4JQ	20 FROM STROUD OR 12 FROM GLOS	STROUD
28	Old Spotted Cow	Marston Meysey	GL11 4JQ	877 CIREN TO LECHLADE	COTSWOLD
29	Plough Inn	Cold Aston	GL54 3BN	801 CHELT TO MORETON	COTSWOLD
30	Prince Albert Inn	Rodborough Hill	GL5 3SS		STROUD
31	Ram Inn	Woodchester	GL5 5EQ	40, 46, 93	STROUD
32	Red Lion	Arlingham	GL2 7JH	113 GLOS TO ARLINGHAM	GLOUCESTER

No.	PUB	ADDRESS	POSTCODE	BUS SERVICES	DISTRICT
33	Rising Sun	Bream	GL15 6JF	73 GLOS TO LYDNEY THEN 727 OR 721	FOREST
34	Royal Oak	Andoversford	GL54 4EH	801 CHELT TO MORETON 853 OXFORD	COTSWOLD
35	Royal Oak	Gretton	GL54 5EP	606 CHELT TO WILLERSEY	COTSWOLD
36	Royal Oak	Painswick	GL6 6QG	46 STROUD – CHELTENHAM	STROUD
37	Salmon	Wanswell	GL13 9SE	207 GLOS TO THORNBURY	GLOUCESTER
38	Salutation Inn	Ham Green	GL13 9QH	207 GLOS TO THORNBURY (BERKELEY)	GLOUCESTER
39	Stagecoach	Newport	GL13 9PY	207 GLOS TO THORNBURY	GLOUCESTER
40	Sun Inn	North Street	GL54 5LH	606 CHELT TO WILLERSEY	COTSWOLD
41	Tipputs Inn	Nailsworth	GL6 0QE	40 STROUD TO WOOTON UNDER EDGE TO HORSLEY. Stop at Bell and Castle and walk up hill.	STROUD
42	Tudor Arms	Slimbridge	GL2 7BP	91 OR 20 TO SLIMBRIDGE CROSSROADS	STROUD
43	Tunnel House	Coates	GL7 6PW	28 CIRENCESTER TO STROUD	COTSWOLD
44	Village Inn	Nailsworth	GL6 0HH	40, 46, 93	STROUD
45	Yew Tree Inn	Clifford's Mesne	GL18 1JS	32 GLOS TO NEWENT THEN 677 OR WALK	GLOUCESTER

Useful Contacts and Websites

Gloucestershire CAMRA
CAMRA is Europe's most successful consumer association, with about 90,000 members. It fights to save Britain's pub heritage and campaigns for a wide choice of tasty traditional beers and ciders.

The Gloucestershire branch now covers the GL postcode area, except the GL54, GL55 and GL56 districts. CAMRA's National Executive recently decided that a separate North Cotswold Branch should be formed to cover the latter districts.
www.gloucestershirecamra.org.uk

Gloucestershire Pubs and Breweries
Gloucestershire Pubs is a website devoted to the history of pubs and breweries in the county. There are over 2,500 pubs listed and described in the 'pub list'. Many of these pubs are now just a distant memory.
www.easywell.co.uk/pubs/

Gloucestershire Tourism
The official website of the Gloucestershire Tourism partnership. Contains detailed information on everything from activities to accommodation. There are a number of links to other useful sites and it is also possible to order online if you would like further information.
www.glos-cotswolds.com

Real Ale in Gloucestershire (RAIG) – an up to date list of real ale pubs throughout Gloucestershire.
www.cauchy.demon.co.uk/raig/guide/GLOS.HTM

Visit the Cotswolds – By Stroud District.
www.visitthecotswolds.org.uk

The Ale Trail Quiz 2008/09

Enjoying the summer outside the Hollow Bottom.

The Ale Trail Quiz 2008/09

This year's competition is a 'pub quiz'.

Visit each of the pubs and find the answer to the questions below. Send in your completed answers on the answer sheets provided *(only answers given on these pages will be entered into the competition)*, and all correct entries will be entered into a draw. Entries for the competition must be received no later than 31 March 2009. The first three fully correct entries drawn will win a prize:

- 1st Prize: 36 pints of beer from each of the 8 Gloucestershire Craft Brewers.*
- 2nd Prize: 18 pints of beer from each of the 8 Gloucestershire Craft Brewers.*
- 3rd Prize: 9 pints of beer from each of the 8 Gloucestershire Craft Brewers.*

*These do not have to be taken and drunk all at once!

GLOUCESTERSHIRE ALE TRAIL QUIZ ENTRY FORM

Name:

Address:

Contact telephone number:

Please send completed entries to Gloucestershire Ale Trail Quiz, c/o 16 Churchill Road, Nailsworth, Stroud, Gloucestershire, GL6 ODL.

TO BE RECEIVED NO LATER THAN 31 MARCH 2009!

	Pub	Quiz Question	Answer
1	Amberley Inn	What does the clock behind the bar say?	
2	Bakers Arms	How many hours did it take to make the rug on the wall?	
3	Bathurst Arms	What make is the log burner at the Bathurst Arms?	
4	Beacon Inn	In which year did The Beacon become a free house?	
5	Bear of Rodborough	Where is the old bell that was used to summon the innkeeper located?	
6	Black Horse	Which hill can be seen the furthest distance from The Black Horse?	
7	Britannia	Name Tina's horse.	
8	Café René	What was René's surname?	

9	Coal House Inn	How many spokes are there in the wheel on the wall of the restaurant?	
10	Corinium Hotel	In which year was the hotel built?	
11	Corner Cupboard Inn	Who slipped in the corner cupboard and in which year?	
12	Craven Arms	How may green bottles are on display in a wall? In the summer you may have to enquire, as they could be covered by a creeper.	
13	Crown & Trumpet Inn	What is the old pub game that is next to the darts board ?	
14	Ebrington Arms	What is the name of the pub dog?	
15	Egypt Mill	Who owns Egypt Mill?	
16	Fiery Angel	Which famous actor is depicted on the door of the gents' loo?	

17	Foston's Ash Inn	Which beef dish is advertised over the bar, but no longer served?	
18	Fountain Inn and Lodge	Which short-lived brewery beer towel hangs on the pub wall?	
19	Gardeners Arms	What is written at the bottom of our mosaic in the garden room?	
20	George Inn	What is the room called to left of the front entrance as you enter?	
21	Hollow Bottom	Whose famous riding saddle is on display in the pub?	
22	Jolly Brewmaster	Who painted the picture?	
23	Kemble Brewery	Which famous royal is pictured drinking a pint at the Kemble?	
24	Mousetrap	What real ale is brewed exclusively for the mousetrap and by which brewery?	

25	New Inn	What originally hung from the hook by the fireplace?	
26	Old Lodge	How many mirrors are there in the 'panel room'?	
27	Old Spot Inn	Which local entrepreneur is in the portrait?	
28	Old Spotted Cow	How many open fires are in the Old Spotted Cow?	
29	Plough Inn	What is the pub dog's name?	
30	Prince Albert Inn	Above the fireplace in The Prince Albert is a large picture. Where would you find an even larger version?	
31	Ram Inn	What year was the pub established?	
32	Red Lion	What makes the bar toilet so unique?	

33	Rising Sun	What is the name of the pub dog and what breed is it?	
34	Royal Oak, Andoversford	Where does time fly backwards?	
35	Royal Oak, Gretton	What is the breed of the pub dog 'Cassie'?	
36	Royal Oak, Painswick	Where would you find Adam and Eve pictured in Paradise?	
37	Salmon	How many wooden posts are on the bar?	
38	Salutation Inn	The pub is part of the Berkeley Estate. Where is the Berkeley Coat of Arms situated within the pub?	
39	Stagecoach Inn	The Stagecoach Inn's name was changed after the Second World War. What was its name before?	

40	Sun Inn	Who signed the electric guitar in the pub?	
41	Tipputs	What is mounted above the fire in the bar?	
42	Tudor Arms	How many real ale pumps are on the bar?	
43	Tunnel House	Which animal is hanging over the fireplace?	
44	Village Inn	In the painting, what is the vicar drinking?	
45	Yew Tree Inn	The Yew Tree sells a bottled cider made in the village. What is it called?	

If you are interested in purchasing other books published by The History Press, or in case you have difficulty finding any books in your local bookshop, you can also place orders directly through our website

www.thehistorypress.co.uk